Looking After Me

Going to

the
Dentist

Sally Hewitt

First published in the UK in 2014 by
QED Publishing
A Quarto Group company
The Old Brewery
6 Blundell Street
London N7 9BH

www.qed-publishing.co.uk

Designed by Astwood Design

A catalogue record for this book is available from the British Library.

ISBN 978 1 78171 552 9

Printed in China

Picture credits
(t=top, b=bottom, l=left, r=right, c=centre fc=front cover)

Shutterstock 4-5 Sergiy Bykhunenko, 6bl Robyn Mackenzie, 6-7 stavklem, 7
Yasonya, 8 wavebreakmedia, 20br donfiore, 22b Lusoimages, 22br Irina Rogova,

Steve Lumb 9, 10, 12, 13, 14-15, 17, 19, 20bl, 21, 22tl, 23

Words in **bold** can be found in the Glossary on page 24

Contents

Healthy teeth

When you smile, people can see your teeth.

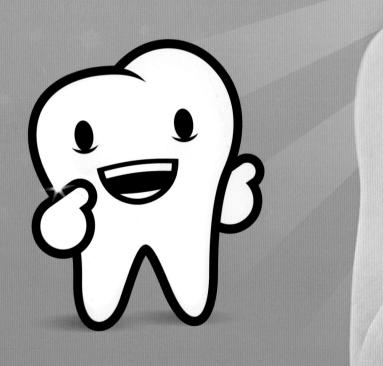

It's lovely if you have a nice smile, with clean, healthy teeth.

Eating fruit and vegetables as a snack is good for your teeth.

"Chomp, Chomp"

"Yum, Yum"

They help to keep your teeth strong and healthy.

Brush your teeth
when you wake up.

Brush them
again when
you go
to bed.

8

Going to the dentist

The **dentist** will help you to look after your teeth.

You need to go to the dentist twice a year.

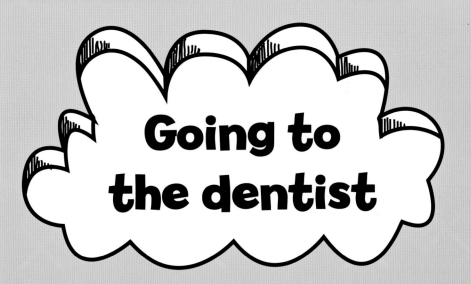

The waiting room

If the dentist is busy, you will have to wait.

You can sit in the waiting room and look at a book.

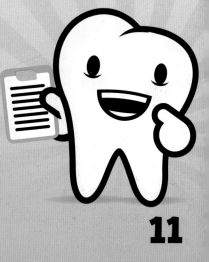

The dentist's chair

The dentist has a special chair for you to sit in. It moves up and down, and can lean back like a bed.

The dentist will give you special glasses to wear. They will **protect** your eyes.

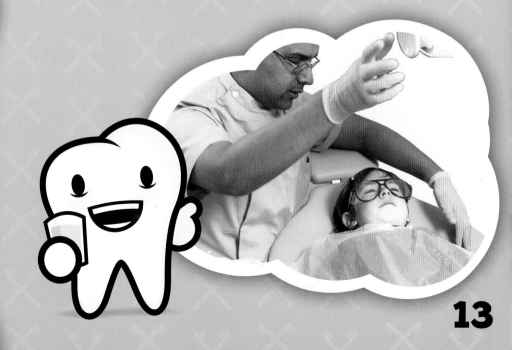

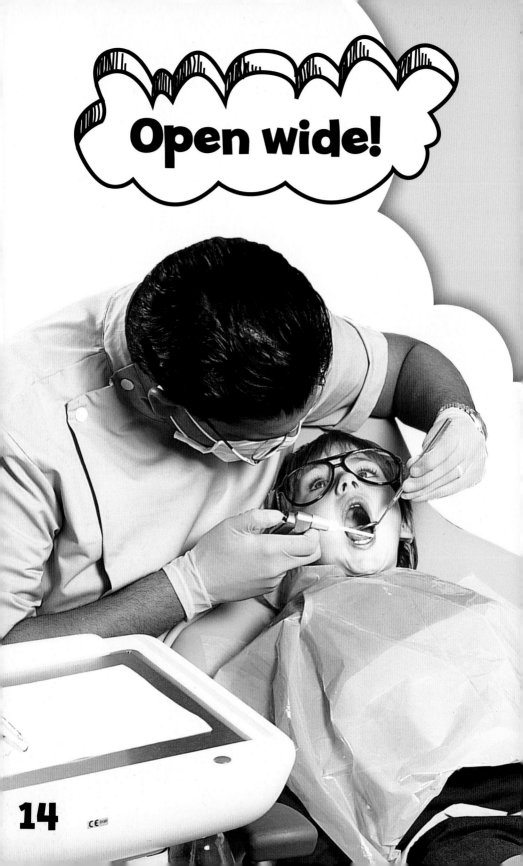

Open wide!

The dentist will ask
you to "open wide!"

Open your mouth
very wide.

The dentist will shine
a light into your mouth.
He will use a small mirror
to look at your teeth.

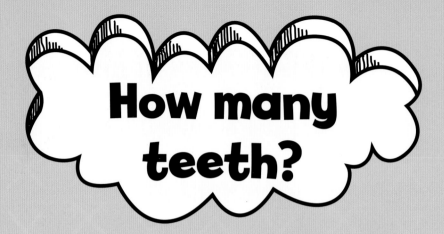

How many teeth?

The dentist will count your teeth.

Have all your **first teeth** grown? If so, you will have ten at the top of your mouth and ten at the bottom.

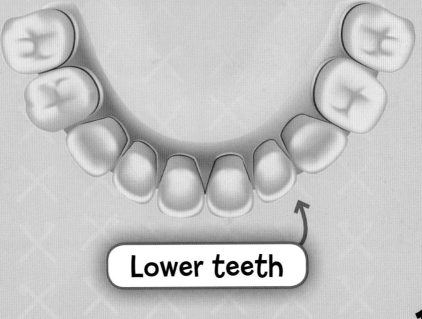

You will have twenty teeth altogether!

Cleaning teeth

The dentist might wash your teeth with water and dry them with a puffer.

The dentist has an electric tool. It buzzes as it cleans and **polishes** your teeth!

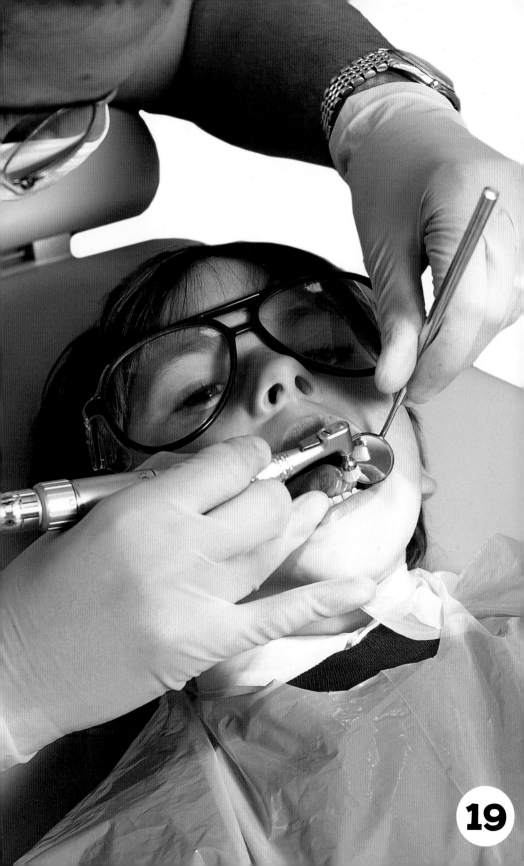

19

Afterwards, you can wash
your mouth with water.

You can spit
the water into
the sink.

Keeping teeth clean

The dentist will show you the best way to brush your teeth.

Try to brush your teeth that way at home.

21

The dentist might give you a pack of things to help you keep your teeth clean

You might even get a sticker, too!

A nice smile

Do you have a small brother or sister? You can show them how to brush their teeth.

Then they will have a nice smile as well.

23

Glossary

dentist   someone who knows a lot about teeth and helps you to keep your teeth strong and healthy

first teeth   the teeth you grow as a baby - they are replaced by grown-up teeth that will last the rest of your life

polish   rub something to make it clean and shiny

protect   keep something safe